What Can You See in This Cloud?

Matt Minshall

OXFORD
UNIVERSITY PRESS

OXFORD
UNIVERSITY PRESS

Great Clarendon Street, Oxford OX2 6DP

Oxford University Press is a department of the University of Oxford.
It furthers the University's objective of excellence in research, scholarship,
and education by publishing worldwide in

Oxford   New York

Auckland   Cape Town   Dar es Salaam   Hong Kong   Karachi
Kuala Lumpur   Madrid   Melbourne   Mexico City   Nairobi
New Delhi   Shanghai   Taipei   Toronto

With offices in

Argentina   Austria   Brazil   Chile   Czech Republic   France   Greece
Guatemala   Hungary   Italy   Japan   Poland   Portugal   Singapore
South Korea   Switzerland   Thailand   Turkey   Ukraine   Vietnam

Oxford is a registered trade mark of Oxford University Press
in the UK and in certain other countries

British Library Cataloguing in Publication Data

Data available

ISBN 978-0-19-919864-1

19 20 18

Printed in China by Imago

Paper used in the production of this book is a natural,
recyclable product made from wood grown in sustainable forests.
The manufacturing process conforms to the environmental
regulations of the country of origin

Acknowledgements

The publisher would like to thank the following for permission to reproduce
photographs: p1 Corel Professional Photos; p2/3 Photodisc/Elements; p4 Matt Minshall (both);
p5 Matt Minshall; p8 Bubbles Photolibrary (bottom), Corel Professional Photos (top);
p9 Matt Minshall; p10 Corel Professional Photos (all); p11 Corel Professional photos (all);
p12 Corel Professional Photos (both); p13 Corel Professional Photos (both); p14 Corbis/
Michael S Yamashita; Corbis/Vladimir Pirogov (top), Getty/Foodpix (centre), Alamy (bottom);
p16 Corbis/Alison Wright (top), corbis/Philip Marazzi (centre), Corbis (bottom left), Corbis/Terry
Whittaker (bottom right); p17 Alamy (top), Matt Minshall (bottom right); Corbis/ David Muench
(bottom left); p18 Alamy; p19 Alamy (top, bottom right and right inset), Corbis/Niall Benvie
(bottom left), Corbis/Wolfgang Kaehler (left inset); p20 Corbis/Cathrine Wessel (top left), Corbis
(bottom left), Corbis/Hal Lott (top right), Alamy (bottom right), p21 Alamy (top), Matt Minshall
(bottom right); Alamy (bottom left); p22 Alamy (both); p23 Still Pictures (top),
Econscene/Melanie Peters (bottom)

Cover photo: Matt Minshall

Illustrations by David Russell

Design by Andy Wilson

Contents

Introduction   4

How the cycle works   6

What are clouds?   8

Cloud shape guide   10

   Low clouds   11

   Medium clouds   12

   High clouds   13

What is water?   14

Precious water   16

Why are trees important?   18

Uses of wood   20

The everlasting cycle   22

Glossary/Index   24

Introduction

Have you ever wondered about the different shapes you can see in clouds? What can these shapes tell us about how those clouds were formed?

Look at this cloud which looks like a camel!

What is the connection between clouds and water? This book will show how they are essential to life on our planet.

Water can also produce amazing shapes, too. What can you see in the water picture here?

These drops of water seen through sunlight look like lumps of molten gold.

What part do trees play in the cycle of life?

The air we breathe, and the constant supply of water in the form of rain, are essential to life on earth.

Trees produce **oxygen**, which we need in order to survive, and they act as filters, cleaning the air that we breathe out. Lots of trees, together in the form of woods and forests, are often called the 'lungs of the earth'. Can you think why?

What can you see in this tree?

There is a natural cycle to life on earth that we can explore through looking at clouds, water and trees.

How the cycle works

Clouds

Clouds appear in many different forms. They can look like beautiful billowing masses of cotton wool in the sky. They can be the dark messengers of coming storms. They can light up as fantastic lightning or crash and bang with noisy thunder. They can also look like peaceful red blankets at the end of a summer's day.

Rain and Water

Each type of cloud gives an idea of what sort of weather to expect. Certain types bring rain, which provides vital water. Rain naturally waters the ground and allows plants to grow. Farmers need rain to grow crops for people and animals.

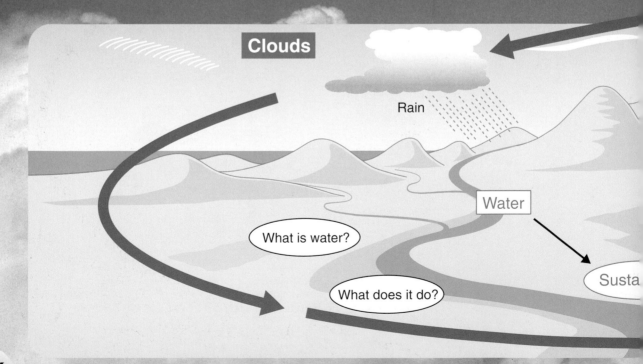

Clouds

Rain

Water

What is water?

What does it do?

Susta

Trees

The biggest and most important plants in this cycle are trees. From trees we get wood, used for paper, furniture, building materials, and boats. In many places, wood is still used for heating and cooking.

Trees produce filtered clean air, and help to form new clouds. Wind or heat causes excess rain water to **evaporate** so that tiny droplets of water mingle with the air. In the right conditions the droplets come together and form clouds once again. They in turn will give the water back to the earth in the form of rain, continuing an everlasting cycle.

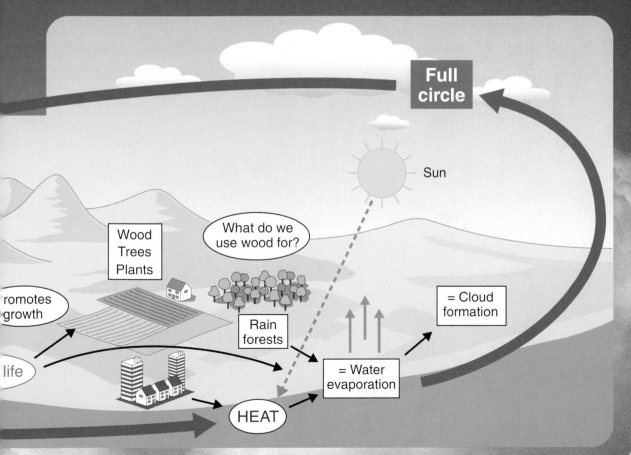

Full circle

Sun

Wood
Trees
Plants

What do we use wood for?

romotes growth

life

Rain forests

= Cloud formation

= Water evaporation

HEAT

What are clouds?

Try this experiment

- Place a glass in the fridge.
- Take it out after 30 minutes and breathe on it.

You should find that a mist appears on the surface of the glass. This is your hot, moist breath meeting the cold surface of the glass. The tiny droplets of water cannot stay separated and are brought together by the cold temperature. This is similar to how clouds are formed.

Clouds are patches of water **vapour** in the air. Water vapour is warm, moist air that we cannot see. When this moist air cools down to the point where it can no longer hold any more water vapour, it produces droplets. After further cooling large amounts of droplets become visible and form big masses which we call clouds.

If you think of what happens to your breath on a cold day, this will help you to understand how clouds are formed.

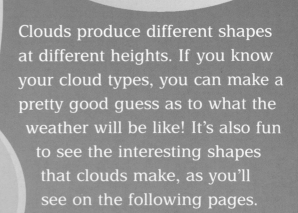

Clouds produce different shapes at different heights. If you know your cloud types, you can make a pretty good guess as to what the weather will be like! It's also fun to see the interesting shapes that clouds make, as you'll see on the following pages.

How do clouds form?

Hot air rises naturally. When a patch of moist air is blown across a warm surface (such as the land after it has been heated by the sun), it is pushed upwards.

Cold air

Clouds form

Meets the cold air

Hot moist air is pushed along by the wind

Hot air rises

Warm surface making the air hot

When the warm air with its evaporated moisture meets the cold air, tiny droplets reform as larger drops that are visible.

This is the start of a cloud.

Hills and clouds

Moist air can also be pushed up as it is blown up the side of a mountain. When it meets colder air high up, it forms clouds. This is known as a 'hill cloud'.

Hill clouds, or Lenticular clouds, are sometimes called wave clouds.

Cloud shape guide

There are three levels of clouds:

Low clouds

These clouds form from up to 2500 metres from the ground.

Medium clouds

These clouds form between 2500–5500 metres from the ground.

Do you think these clouds look like small bits of cotton wool?

High clouds

These clouds form between 5500–12 000 metres from the ground.

Do you think these clouds look like cotton wool dipped in grey ink?

What do you think these ones look like?

Low clouds

Fog and mist are low clouds, which form on or very near the ground, if the air is moist and cold enough. Low clouds are normally the ones that bring rain, sleet, hail, snow, thunder and lightning.

Fracto clouds are small bits of cloud that have not yet formed into cumulus clouds. They are normally associated with nice weather.

Fracto clouds

Small cumulus clouds

The base of these clouds is wider than the height. They are normally called fair weather clouds.

Cumulonimbus (Cu-nimb for short)

These are known as thunderclouds. Thunder, lightning and rain is highly likely – take your umbrella!

Large cumulus clouds

These are great billowing clouds. The height of these clouds is longer than the base. The weather will probably be fine, but take a raincoat, just in case!

Medium clouds

Some medium clouds that are high up are composed of ice particles. Medium clouds sometimes have the prefix 'alto'.

Alto-cumulus

These clouds indicate weather that is dry and overcast, but can be messengers of bad weather to come.

Altostratus

These clouds mean that the weather will get colder.

High clouds

High clouds have the prefix 'cirro', and are so high that they are composed only of ice particles.

Cirrus clouds are often called Mares' Tails. Can you see why?

Cirrus clouds are thin and wispy. There is a possibility of high winds on the way, but they can also mean stable weather for a while.

Cirro-cumulus clouds may mean a storm, but could mean stable weather for the moment.

Cirro-cumulus clouds are sometimes called 'mackerel skies' as the pattern looks a bit like the skin of a mackerel.

'Mackerel skies and mares' tails make tall ships shorten sails'. This is an old sailing proverb – what do you think it might mean?

What is water?

From clouds comes water, which falls as rain, hail, sleet and snow.

What is water?

Water is made up of two gases – **hydrogen** (H) and oxygen (O), and is scientifically referred to as H_2O, which means that there are two parts of hydrogen to each part of oxygen.

Water, water everywhere

Water is the most common **compound** on the Earth. It covers nearly three-quarters of the earth's surface. However, most of it is in the form of sea water which is salty and undrinkable.

We need water for survival and it is important that it is clean. If water is dirty with pollution or poisons, then we can become ill and may die. Many people in the world cannot get clean water easily and so suffer from thirst or disease.

Why do we need water?

85% of our bodies are made up of water. We need water for our bodies to work properly. We lose water from sweating and going to the loo and we must replace it. We need about 1–1$\frac{1}{2}$ litres (or 9 glasses) of water per day, but if the weather is hot, we may need as much as 2$\frac{1}{2}$ litres (or 15 glasses).

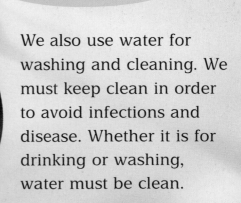

We also use water for washing and cleaning. We must keep clean in order to avoid infections and disease. Whether it is for drinking or washing, water must be clean.

Precious water

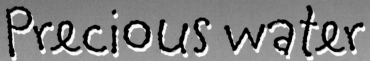

Water gives life to every living thing on the earth. From ants to roses to oak trees to elephants, they all need water. Did you know that everything you eat has also needed water at some time in its growth cycle?

How does pollution affect our water?

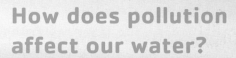

Pollution comes from poisons that we produce, such as car exhaust gases, which get into the air and make their way into rain through the water cycle. The waste from chemical factories is often dumped straight into rivers making the water dangerous for fish, humans and sometimes plants and trees.

Water images

Water can produce wonderful images. What can you see in these pictures?

Why are trees important?

Clouds drop water in the form of rain. Water makes plants grow. There are thousands of different plants. The most important plants in the cycle are trees. They play a key role in our survival. The leaves of a tree take in the air that we breathe out (**carbon dioxide**), along with some of the fumes produced by cars, and change them into pure oxygen. We breathe in this 'clean' air, which allows us to live and thrive.

Trees have either hard wood or soft wood and can be classed into two groups:

- deciduous – the leaves of these types of trees appear in spring and summer and are lost in the autumn and winter;

- evergreens – these trees appear to keep their leaves all through the year. However, each leaf sheds itself and a new one replaces it, but not in time with the seasons. This gives the impression of the trees being covered in leaves all year round.

OXYGEN

TREES

CARBON DIOXIDE

Deciduous trees

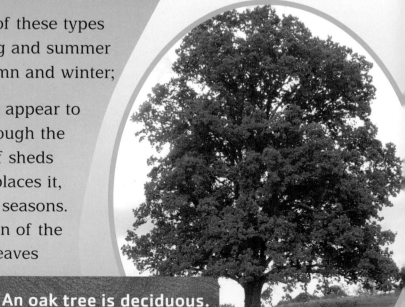

An oak tree is deciduous.

Willow branches make the best arrows because they are straight and smooth.

Evergreen trees

Ginkgo trees come from China and their leaves are used as medicine.

Scots Pines grow very quickly so are used to make furniture.

Did you know that the hair of sumo wrestlers in Japan is tied in the shape of a Ginkgo leaf?

Uses of wood

Have you ever thought of what wood can be used for? Although metals and plastics are used for many things, wood is still used for some everyday things.

Furniture

Many people still use open fires for cooking and for warmth. More wood is used for fires than any other use.

Firewood

Think how much furniture such as chairs, tables, chests of drawers, cupboards, and sideboards is made from wood.

Paper

Building materials

The roofs, walls and floors of many buildings use wood.

After fires, the most use made of wood is for paper. Every day forests of an area the size of 100 000 football pitches are cut down to make paper. That is why it is important to recycle paper to help protect the Earth's forests.

Filling up with a tree ...?

If trees are left to rot naturally they simply become part of the earth. If the land changes suddenly, due to a violent earthquake or a volcanic eruption covering a forest, the trees can remain as they are under a layer of earth or lava. After many thousands of years they turn first into coal and then into oil. These are used to produce fuel, petrol and **diesel**.

Images in wood

Like clouds and water, wood can produce some startling images. Trees themselves can be interesting shapes. The details of the bark and grain of the wood when it is cut can also show some surprising images. What can you see in these?

The everlasting cycle

Clouds are important because they give us rain. Rain water keeps us alive by providing drinking water. It supports the growth of plants to feed us and trees from which we get wood to use for warmth, shelter, cooking, paper and furniture. Some water evaporates back into the air where it once again forms clouds.

To make sure that this everlasting and incredible cycle continues, we must ensure our Earth's water is kept clean, forest **felling** is controlled and that we recycle the things we use as much as possible.

Glossary

alto – Latin for 'high' but used to prefix Medium clouds

carbon dioxide – a colourless gas formed when breathing

compound – a mixture of two or more things

diesel – the fuel used for diesel engines, made from oil

evaporate – to turn from liquid or solid into vapour

fell – to cut down

hydrogen – a colourless and tasteless gas. It is the lightest of all elements and is found in water and all livings things

oxygen – a gas found in water and air essential to our survival

vapour – moisture or other substance suspended in air such as mist or smoke

Index

alto-cumulus clouds 12
altostratus clouds 12
cirro-cumulus clouds 13
cirrus clouds 13
coal and oil 21
compound 14
cumulonimbus 11
cumulus 11
deciduous trees 18
diesel 21
evergreen trees 18–19
firewood 20
fog 11
fracto clouds 11
growth cycle 16
high clouds 10, 13
hill cloud 9
hills 9
hydrogen 14
lenticular (wave) cloud 9
low clouds 10–11
medium clouds 10, 12
mist 11
moisture 9
oxygen 5, 14
paper 20
petrol 21
pollution 17
rain 6, 7, 11, 14, 18, 22
trees 5, 7, 18–19, 20, 21
water 4, 6–7, 14, 15, 16, 17
water cycle 17
water vapour 7, 8, 9
weather 8, 11, 12, 13
wood 20, 21